仁

What reviewers have said about Janet Charman's work ...

In her laconic and original style, Janet Charman writes a body of work that sees [her] exploiting the motif of journeying to investigate the colonised land, past and present. – Siobhan Harvey, *Landfall 225*, p. 182

Charman's project is 'activating a small moment', unfolding from the slightest fragment of daily minutiae a sense of miracle: bliss is localised, transcendence is brief and raw, insight comes from focusing on the base elements of an average life ... – Tracey Slaughter, *Landfall 214*, p. 170

Charman's verse has always been distinguished by a combination of astute observation, compassion, pluck, vulnerability and willingness to poke fun at herself. – Iain Sharp, *Sunday Star-Times*, 20 July 2008

仁surrender

janet charman

OTAGO UNIVERSITY PRESS

Published by Otago University Press
Level 1, 398 Cumberland Street
Dunedin, New Zealand
university.press@otago.ac.nz
www.otago.ac.nz/press

First published 2017

ISBN 978-1-98-853110-6

A catalogue record for this book is available from the National Library of New Zealand.

Editor: Anna Hodge

Front cover photo: Max White, *Lantern Festival, Auckland*, 2010
Back cover author photo: Max White

Printed in New Zealand by Printlink Ltd, Wellington.

contents

to *my* room nineteen

narrow entrance with a plumbed annexe for waste and wash
other side cupboards hold a felt carpeted box
with a pin number under which vibrate my passport and an envelope of
    cash
twice daily i kneel in this vestibule
to roll wrung garments in a dry towel
hang damp things on an elastic i've strung
between the pole of the permanently open closet
and the meeting suite's locked communicating door

duck under my line
to come further in

the corner shelf
where cases dragged through travel filth
are reefed on the filthy case-mat
i've redesignated
clean space
since the red hand towel
in which he insisted i wrap my laptop
is spread over it

and there i've settled the kettle and cups
teabag eyes
orange nose
golem of banana fingers
electric currant biscuits

when i arrived twin beds stuck into the room
i couldn't rest
it takes a sizable chunk of the first night
to ease their erections into an L
one crisp moonlight stripe duvet
out-spread
the other in a plumped roll

and placing the bedside cabinets so
no one should bang their head
on the wall-mounted lamps

in this furniture shifting
the telephone cord tension hastily slackened
your time three a.m.
my time my own

cinnamon wool blankets
found on the hallway shelf
draped
to make the beds say just enough
O so busy dawn to dusk with this

at the desk my internet linked up
and above the fridge
the TV nattering on like an old school friend

as i hang damp trousers from the ledge above the window-bay
the air-conditioning cables lodged there fall away

the view of the university
building over the road
the views of the apartment blocks on the hillside
the views of the email
the view of the sky

Hallelujah!
the telephone ringing
you want my opinion
about a translation you're making

i tighten my lava-lava
and answer the door of my poem

in you come
and draw the curtains:
but who was watching?
i keep them open

where people are

1. alive in jewelled walls
i am a new arrival to this cabinet on the ninth floor
a grey crab immobilised in twine
yet a few evenings later i'm rattling round
like an almond in a drawer
then every morning when i scuttle out the weather has grown colder
the newspaper says they've opened nine chill shelters for the homeless
i peer down to ground level
and decide from passers-by if i'll need long sleeves
each day it's freezing

cloud shadows pass
palm leaves gust
see how these tremors manifest on the ceiling

at a window across the valley an inhabitant leans out
an eleven second story to pull in her quilt

i am that chopstick that fell from the table
i am that chewed bone left on the cloth
though as i'm beginning to form an opinion
you'll see me in the lotus-shaped bowl they're filling
with green tea for sterilising

a restaurant utensil
plunged to wash off
any microscopic bit of stuck-on sediment
the dishwasher didn't get at

our graceful host makes her gestures apt
to fit this vessel
which is up to just below overflowing

that's me
not quite spilling

and before we eat i arm myself
against too much relief at your acceptance
since i am the battle that wants to be fought
but when you say you like what i write
and in your translation
my lesbian allusion
is colloquially rendered 'female comrade'
i become the big messy nest of an unknown bird
found all along the highway between Qufu and Mount Tai on The
    Mainland

no one can tell me what name that bird has or where it has flown
though it knows

is it centred from a hide in your web pages?
is it scavenging my Octopus card in the MTR?

anyhow
if you think now you can leave me alone
to get on with my independent learning
think again
i am actually a left margin justified crazy person
who agitating at her map in the crowded concourse
will talk to herself
and wheeling down the mountain
i am the green sweep of the mendicant's robe
drink in his tragic theatre
his rictus of despair
whatever
not giving any money to a beggar
i am that woman

eventually able
to get relief
but high on Mount Tai one who no longer expects
that where we eat
there'll automatically be a place to piss

and now i'm also understanding
how expectation makes me ridiculous

when we get to The Mainland you switch
and i digest
that since we met you've been speaking to me in a foreign language

i
think
women
communicate
with men about sex
in a language
foreign
to us

can you say if you really wanted me to take up your invitation
for the massage you mentioned?
and when our feet no longer ached would it be
finished? at that time of night
with her last clients
while we head off to dinner
must this masseuse accept some chilly weight?
until she gets her ride home late
that's what would happen where i come from
but in your *Microcosmos*
the lines of towels of all sizes that hang outside the massage house
are readied for a speech contest
good strong boy-towels wagging the breeze

'where are all the girl-towels?'
trust me to ask

soaking

imagine them
consonant dancers

a rainbow serpent   stretching a circle
in the soft   smooth-flowing   water

2. with daylight
i am becoming
another woman
chosen for smiling in the cold at reception
but however tall i appear in my boots and red coat my shift is longer

i am the parts of many dishes
left on the table when the guests have finished
i am your beloved wife's voice in the distance
i am the grey Mainland preparing urgently for transfiguration by
    Capitalism
i have not looked at my hands but they may need scrubbing
and regular four-hourly disinfection

i am the wrinkled shirt where the sweat smells like deodorant
i am our unexpected stopovers
i am the line of wash you dodge to come into my room
i am the dragon eyes of the smoke detector
which are opening and closing
they have seen everything
and many times over

where you hold tight to the handrail i am the precipice you are close to
i am your sensational mouth
i am that day when in our arms for the first time we held our daughters
i'm the friend – mortally ill – who has flown from this country
to be with his family
and die in mine

i am the youth by the fire extinguisher in the moving train
who holds on to his girlfriend as if no one can see them

i am the sex goddess who uses Botox
i am the Men's Fun business

i am the boy in the little club shooting up
in the dark
i am the one who has that touch holds down a heart
and wants that talk which opens the door to another time zone

when the answer is no
i am the one who doesn't hear so well
whose content
is in our books
leaning together
in the light of the verandah

who waits to ask about your cough
whose teabag lasts for three cups
who wants to be civil to your wife and her parents
and would like to like her better than either of us

sometimes i can make the audience laugh
but here i am annoying the journalism students with a long poem that is
not
topical enough

i am but one whose work you've translated
who you pushed to the edge and from whom you retreated
who fears men for every good reason
and still wants to be wrong about them

your poem conversation with a lover – embracing her
silence
i am the one who broke in asking
that this consummation
should be reopened

when you put the rowdy guest out of your house and won't let her back
i am the one under a full moon
howling

i am the one on The Mainland walking
in a decorated face mask with her boyfriend
and he
since they are a couple
expects to pay
for everything
and she is going to marry him on an auspicious date to be announced
soon
but there is still time

i am the one who showers considerately at night for her family
and arrives at work in the morning a little bit sweaty
who knocks a knob on her room phone and starts a siren
who you found in a struggle with the hairdryer
because it won't turn off
and you hang it up to make it stop
telling me developing countries don't have off switches

then just at the moment someone compliments me yet again on my left-
handed dexterity
i am the one whose piece of crispy duck splashes onto the tablecloth

i am the life-size replica of Margaret Thatcher
hunched forward attending the words of Deng Xiaoping
in the *Century of China* exhibition at the Hong Kong History Museum i
am enjoying
his nonchalant posture

i am the people jam for The Peak Tram
my Comrade friend was born up here many years before The Handover
above the view i listen for her
first cry

i am the *Häagen-Dazs* mascarpone ice-cream i ate
twice
that one of the staff asked me how to pronounce

but what would i know? since i am the one frozen to the bone at Lantau
who you insisted should try
hot black
sesame soup

it is
delicious

and then you command me to lay off the soy sauce
which overpowers all the other flavours

intermittently out of the mist
The Buddha appears
very trim at two hundred and fifty metric tonnes

once i saw some women at our airport greet their newly arrived priest
with joyful obeisance
to the side on a bench the European devotee
half perched
with the car keys

receiving a blow
if you've forgotten what happened the bruises know

in the cold gondolas
i am the one who suspects you feel vertigo

and so i can please get some sleep
i want this crush on you to be over

when you said you could see more people
should read my work
that was the aphrodisiac

but why praise my style by publicly quipping
that in comparison your own is nothing?
some have greatness thrust upon 'em

you give me your selected poems

– uncrush this a little
my friend i've read them

you are nothing

as the air is

i'm breathing

did you think i'd expire when i find you're a lyre?
no fear
you inspire

i dare say we're both liars

3. not forgetting
i am the one whose other life waits
out there
like an indigenous owner
holding on
for the return of their home
like The Mainland
holding on
for the return of Taiwan
here i am
the one sniffing these other writers' successes
most indecorous

at the back of my notebook i make dozens of jottings
leaving room at the front
for important thoughts
but never have any

and till the market women run after me pleading i am the one afraid to
bargain

who purchases sundry fridge magnets and three acrylic-blend pashminas
for which i can honestly say no endangered species gave up their fleeces

in that very local way
i am the one who agonises over the democratic politics
of giving presents
what to give
to whom and when
with what wrappings and un-wrappings
what to make of the photo opportunities
that spring from these
spontaneous demonstrations

the one who wants to live in a place like this
where students walk from satellite campuses
in sub-zero temperatures
to hear a poet like you warm us through
but because these enclave streets are clearer
on account of the armed guards at the entrances
and exits
i don't want to stay on The Mainland either

then when your airport shuttle is due
i am the one who waits for you
on the last couch
with a gift for your spouse
presumptuous
this wrap – should she receive it –
as the calculation of a Mrs Ferrars
or the kindness of a Mrs Jennings

and now you're on your way home
i see how you can look after a good night's sleep
you give me your hand with its heat
you are not a photograph in my brain
yet
my voice is wobbling

i hurry off to get it hidden in Pacific Coffee
which is closed
it must be Sunday
i try the dining hall on Baptist University Road
where i choke on my food
and leave it uneaten
but that's not your pigeon
i've run out of protease inhibitions

i gulp my way down the hill
to the Kowloon Tong station
at least i know where this curved white avenue is leading
walking it like stroking the little bit grubby limbs of a long-legged
    European

at a roller-door phone i'm passing a young speaker is saying
'i am the elocution teacher'
and they buzz her in
that's what i have become
somebody waiting for anyone who'll buzz her in
because English here is but one swift current bound in the Cantonese
    ocean

despite that
while we were stuck in The Olive Basket transit café at the airport
en route from The Mainland
i tried for a piece of your sweet tanghulu

and even if we don't collaborate
like you first suggest
i insist
that despite your objections
i would know what to do

you say these particular characters
are each suspended in a multi-level narrative
which can't be interpreted into English

my answer is i'd intuit
bite through them
bit by bit
if you'd explain
i can do it

now you down my questions
saying your text doesn't stack up in any manner for a language outsider
to comprehend it
– not even if you sent me the words
after your Other Half has seen them into English?
– not even with the way the whole of the two of you
make one of them?
no
the ideas would be attenuated
but i don't want to accept that
and since i'm older it takes more people to push me over
hers is another voice i'd like to encounter

4. okay then
i'll admit it
work in translation can be leaden
yet
in her rendition your poems
are incandescent
fired from one language to another
read on a dark night
seen ever after
in their own light
but here your pouring thoughts call for surrender
my head on this table – so keep your 'nocturnal emissions'
call them starlight
if anyone can transcend the subtextual comic inflections
you can
i can't resist you
i want your attention

but please
i don't want to be produced
with a man's hand angling my head
like in the Judd Apatow in-flight comedy i saw on my way back
where he's saying 'this is Hollywood
swallow it'

and that tip tapping
isn't the sound of a chorus line
it's my keyboard's finger sequencing

but now i'm getting it in the neck
from those sextras i was appraising
in the gangster movie pole-dance scene
on TV
they've come down to the front of the screen
and begun appraising
me
but aren't those fully dressed men the ones they should be questioning?
and all the directors? who've set them up
as fuck furniture

in truth
those women were with me in the transit café at the airport
because in my head
among the dead of the coffee cups
i felt naked
risking one harsh second-to-last laugh the universe was having
at the fact our worlds were set
to fly apart
and despite that
i was out there trying to catch your drift
for the sixtieth time in a month
and i want to put that in italics
but i haven't

and there goes your language up and down and across in strokes of glyph
music

even to where
reading it through stinging particles of notes in English
i find my hair standing on end
even to where
because you've kept me at a distance
it's like being in The Catholic Church
and having to hear all those common-sense words of rejection
The Holy Fathers offer up
in the language of running
nits and pricking
for what's feminine and i evade them
to listen to your arias
and take the tanghulu into my mouth

chew through
piece by piece
to my sense of refreshment
as you relent
and show me where you've cracked the sugar
in the restored walls of The Confucian Mausoleum

this poem
you're planning
takes me straight
to the tart fruit
i want

if i grasp

your intention

that The Direct Descendants' Family Name
be transfigured
as a place for women
reclaiming
their private
part

they who
through
what you call the small hole of the feminine
shall make a place to
raise up

but here
i am
making my stand on the grounds of the clitoral
shaken
out
where winds drown
or carry my voice
will you hear my shout?
that in these phoenix arts
one wit isn't enough

you decide

hard by your depiction
i say men have holes
might make them receptive as anything women commission
is the private part entered solely in the feminine?
render the private part surrendered in the masculine

where bees figure in the honey
let them

but i am for a morning sunlit beyond planting
good green filth
that sugar snap i get from red work
where the almonds of the earth break into leaf
this is the fifth season
not a revolution
a hole in the real
where any body might encounter the generative-feminine

make your embrace that poem

5. yet i fear
with things as they are
i will have to make do
with clopping down the vagina-walled avenue
to the Confucius Family tomb
the donkey drawing our party through
as the whip cracks across her old shoulders
– the carter's three-year-old nephew borne there
falling asleep on his feet
and then we leave him at the gates of the garden of death
transfer to a minivan to get to the main graves
buried among pine forest
no bird or serpent or girl permitted to live
here where The Red Guard came
savaging

and later at the hotel you give me the sharp of your tongue
because you know it never even occurred to me
to bring an electronic dictionary
Western cultural hegemony
you exercise your right to be angry
yes i'm ashamed
still i presume
to take the tanghulu into my mouth

'cunt' and 'Kant' you remark
who may use language like that?
– poets! it is our categorical imperative

i say: 'wǔdǎyī' and 'Huáyǔ'
somebody! with a point of view

and with tongues Lu Xun'd
what more unforeseeable vocabulary could be spat between us?

in my notebook
you write: 'bitter' 'pizza'
and think of cutting short your trip
abandoning ship

but i intend to wade in
test with my thumb like a blind person
find where the ink has risen
and fill my pen

then you arrive from another direction
require me to consider
what will be left of the Chinese culture
when Capitalism has finished planting its landscapes with Coca-
Cola

and yet
i can still argue
that there are numbers of us
coming out of the family whole
to the hill of the clitoris
and somebody else at Mount Tai told us: 'observances are being made here
to the Grandmother's Grandmother'

that head view happening
as i look at the mountain
which you conceded was culturally significant
but not
on a five
yuan
note
particularly interesting

well
that's true
not interesting in comparison with the strokes of the naked man we saw
swimming in the reservoir
as it started snowing on our way down

    in your home town
    you said
    he would have been arrested

or the black swan
which is how i've been thinking of one of the women
who was with me when she lit her incense packet
the scent ascending as we prepared to climb higher
'i never know how to make observances' she mutters
my answer: be who we are
perhaps the smoke will wind round our bodies and make us happier?
then as i clamber up the steps i spare an arrow
for the woman guard doing pat-down searches all day at the Mainland
border
who pinched my genitalia
– that she will find better things to do with her fingers

and that we'll enter
not
into revolution together
but rather that your audacious configurations
will deliver to us so many good reasons
why the infant in the covered wagon
who rode with us to the funeral gates
might re-encounter his m/Other
and live some ways we are not required to answer: 'i am ab*so*lute*ly
sweet!'
as the cane beats the sugar into us

our guide explained that ancient torture
showed us
the raised platform ridged for knees
where they flogged kneeling men
where they flogged kneeling women
whatever they were feeling
under threat of execution
required to keep smiling

in New Zealand we had judicial floggings
until 1935

but what i have
here
is your voice
dismantling the walls of conformity

a woman breathing in

and in
her arms
of language

the weight of a poetics
which brings to consciousness
the blush of the body joyous

and everywhere
people are
we know
there is more
of this

Wo de tian a!

My Sky O! – Good Heavens!

in the visitors' booklet it says Che Kung Temple
is dedicated to a Song Dynasty general
will i see anything
other than by leaving my room?
becoming a map spider
who scuttles through Lok Fu station
navigating into a seat for The New Territories
and when i get off the train
there are the tourist point signs
going into the tiled tunnel
i head under the traffic
to the highway's other side
and along Tai Chung Kiu Road
ask two women outside the gateway 'is this the temple?'
'yes' they say
and stalk down before me
through the covered wooden entrance
bounded by cabinets full of bunches of incense
for purchase
and one small carved-wood dragon
in my imagination
a manifestation of The Rainbow Serpent
price on application?
not for sale

then i go around the side of the building
in search of a toilet
and find one out the back of a rattan-roofed dining room
where several cats are meditating among the chair legs
by the tap
where i wash my hands
there's liquid soap
then it's back
to the front steps

where i climb up
to the next level
past the crudely concreted ramp
for differently abled and stroller access
and in the centre of the upper courtyard
find a life-size representation of an entity
who may be feminine
and who has stiff porcelain robes
blown into folds
with joss sticks set about
and the office women i saw before
are circling the figure
kneeling every so often
in their zip suits
and city boots
very focused
with packets of lit incense
making their observances

i sit down
on a step against a shed wall
and for my sore back take two Panadol
it's not too hot
in fact
as i close my eyes and lean against the wood
all the days of the week recede
and the sun shining
makes me sleepy
i get up then
go out to the street
decide to walk on as far
as round the corner
where i discover the as-advertised temple
the immense
multi-courtyard one for The General
containing a five-times-height statue of him looking fierce and clasping a big sword

so i go in the other direction
to the Hong Kong Heritage Museum
and when i get in there
my back is hurting again
so i can't be bothered with the ceramics exhibition
i take the escalators all the way to the top floor so i won't have to think
and find at the last stop they have an installation called *Happy Fruit*
into which i traipse
because it's free
and it turns out to be
about a woman called Lydia Sum
who was a big Hong Kong identity
in every sense of the word
but she's died recently
and here on display are all her costumes
sequin and ostrich-feather outfits with heels to match
and every single frock makes me feel like a million dollars
is the wrong equation for how we absorb the feminine
since each piece is alive with jouissance
then when i get back to the hotel i mention what i saw to one of the others
and she tells me Lydia Sum was sometimes referred to as 'Fatty'
affectionately
and i want to burst into tears

they say you're Japanese

and are
from Okinawa
though actually
when we get right down to it
you were born on Ishigaki
in the archipelago of Ryukyu in Urumanesia
and the presence of American bases
occupying 20 per cent of your main island
is a stone in your shoe

tonight in the Wonderland restaurant
we begin to talk
and write down words for each other when the ideas aren't clear
like Māoritanga
and how as long as i can remember
and before
the tangata whenua in Aotearoa have fought to be rid of European power

our intermarriage
their embarrassing indigenous tent embassies at Parliament
their hīkoi
their sit-ins
their occupations
their whakapōhane
their seminars for oblivious Feminists and Christians
their anguished histories and submissions to social and cultural
    institutions
their relentless efforts to revive te reo
their defiant arts
their warrior sports
their unenforceable treaty
their prolonged attempts to halt land alienation
their arrests and court cases and interminable imprisonments
their devastated families
their television appearances

as if you don't know
on the plane returning from Shandong i tell you
and how Māori Party representative Hone Harawira's email leaked this
 week says:
'White motherfuckers have been raping our lands and ripping us off for
 centuries'
that's when i feel
your palpable withdrawal
in Ryukyu
where it's as assimilatively true
from the beginning
you've told me
religious authority
has been transmitted through the crowns of women
and in one book you've written there is a photograph of your mother
at the temple where she ministered
and people came to her
to have their life's work consecrated

once at home i was walking up our Queen Street
to the casino
and met Hone Harawira
who saw i'd recognised him
and he gave me a big smile
as you do
here
whenever your English evaporates

but i notice
that at times
when i'm lost or disoriented
you navigate these streets effortlessly
and one day
you spelled out for us
your belief that in a multicultural situation
what matters most
isn't understanding
but respect

every day from your house you say you can hear the waves
breaking on the reef

Everything Congee

Jinan City is fogged in
we get rerouted to Hefei
which by the way
through the freezing breakfast-room window
is mourning grey
with masked men and women streaming down the overpass to work
whereas at night
venturing out in my puffy coat
this icy street has its own atmosphere of lit particulate
wherein i catch you two poets shooting 'lonesome man' photos
each for the other coming humbly to attention
in the camera's record of our stranding in the industrial borderlands
'but we haven't had dinner!'
plaintive geese round the corner
forgoing street food to sit together in a dim white gloom
attached
to the merest gesture of a kitchen
from which we eat the requisite famine-defying courses: rice vegetables
    fish pork
then we go in the dark for a walk with the writer whose home to the west
is just a hundred and thirty Ks away – say Auckland to Whangarei
fate has thrown him
onto the doorstep of his own grand city: Nanjing
but he chooses to remain with us
in this obscure place
whose population is the same as my entire nation
our guide past a store little wider than a bedroll where
in her stylist's chair the proprietor is settling herself for the night
and thence we troop into the last open shop
where three camouflage fashionistas are soaking their feet in bowls of hot
    water
placed in the aisles between piles of fur ear-flap hats and padded jackets
    and fashion
victim bullet-proof vests and olive-drab soldier caps with single red stars
    at the front

but as they start to lock up we're decanted into the street
where we re-encounter the lonesome poets
you direct us
to go in and eat some congee in the Everything Congee Restaurant
although
we're not
terribly
hungry
we acquiesce
mine is
the savoury dish
which sticks to my ribs
and though it tastes of green beans in liquefied sun
is so big
i can't finish

my Korean is better

that's what's you say
wherever
whenever
you are expected to speak English
and when i first saw you
i thought you walked like the 'Staying Alive' character
in *Saturday Night Fever*
and then you told us a bit
about what it was like growing up on the DMZ
in a military family
and the fires they set to eat up the grass in no man's land
so the soldiers along the frontier can keep eyeballing each other
and of the coal stove poison gases that felled you and your mother
who after she came round in the hyperbaric chamber
discovered you were alive in there with her
and later she realised that all the memories you had
the day before they put you in
were gone
ten years of them
and after that i didn't tend to notice how you walked
so much as the unscheduled detours you took
bringing stories back
through cities and airports
for instance
that tale of the once-a-year ritually bathing nuns
but it's not so easy for me
to put on paper
what you convey about them in conversation
forty religious
soaking up in Japan
because where i come from
at public baths
women
and men
are obliged to wear swimming costumes

and then you mention the impromptu gathering that happens
on maids-day-off Sundays in Hong Kong
Philippines women
who meet at the plaza
and no matter what passing shoppers are thinking
start dancing together
and singing
and i also got told
by somebody else
about an employer who would climb on a chair
to smack her maid in the face
but you weren't there when i heard about that
it was from some European expats
one of whom has been trying to help this young servant
get her life back
but things seem to be going from bad to worse
men and so forth
well
i also have to mention
that novel passage they accidentally translated
which you hadn't intended
about one of your characters procuring for herself
a nihilistic sexual climax
you'd actually indicated to them for translation
the piece right after this
where the guys in the blizzard
talk to the taxi driver
but the student who tore off your good bit
seemed utterly confident with its sexual content
and so were the audience of mainly female Mainland students
who gave your words the undivided attention you'd expect
from listeners who may have had cause
from time to time
to participate
for ourselves
in quite a few
hundred

thousand
nihilistic sexual climaxes
not to mention a handful or so of the other
more sociable kind
and when you confide your confusion
about the extract the student has chosen
you add the disclaimer
that when you wrote that section
you were young and full of testosterone
which brings the house down
after that
you went ahead in Korean
and read us the part you'd really chosen
regarding the blizzard
and those guys
talking their way through it

it’s late

it’s late in the café on Festival Walk at the back of the Agnès B boutique
the men have coffee and insist on paying for the women’s desserts
in the raspberry ice i taste the thin red stripe of your fleecy shirt
is like a pyjama top i once had but on you it fits in that very arresting XY shape
that goes with the James Dean cut of your leather jacket
which has the zip-out inner for when the weather goes below freezing
and this is how it might’ve looked on JD if he’d been smart enough to get older
and write novels and scripts and live on The Mainland
and the two of you could be giving up the smokes together
but one time when i was bleeding to death
yes yes bleeding to death
i said to my baby’s father ‘please stop with the cigarettes’
thinking our children would be half orphans
and he being their sole parent
would need to stick around as long as possible to support their lives without me
but his reply was: ‘i can’t’
well
that was that
until fifteen years later just before the cancer he read Allen Carr’s
Easy Way to Stop Smoking
and quit
but it isn’t available in Mandarin although they’d make millions and millions
out of a translation
i mean here they smoke in the lifts they smoke look i smoked myself for two
weeks in 1972 and i still inhale on finger cigarettes if i’m driving alone feeling like shit

on the sliding rack

> *The Shanghai Panda Dairy is closed again for milk powder containing melamine.*
> – Agence France-Presse report, 2 January 2010

on the sliding rack
behind the couch in the foyer
hoist like a flag
the *South China Morning Post*
while i wait
i read its front-page snippet about the execution for melamine contamination
of Zhang Yujun and Geng Jinping
a dairy farmer and a salesperson
and the lifetime imprisoning of Tian Wenhua
Sanlu dairy company chairwoman

when i fed my babies
milk came out of my breasts in sprays
not like from a tap
more like rain in the mouth
and on my chest of drawers there's a pulse of those dots i've never washed off

do you think that's disgusting?

the ten thousand New Zealand dairy farmers who own Fonterra
had a 43 per cent stake in Sanlu
today they are being urged to supplement their co-op shares
by managers who want to take the dairy giant multinational
and fully maximise its potential
the way the big boys do
Fonterra management knew on the second of August 2008
that our milk was poisoned
but the first official communication about it
from New Zealand to the Chinese

Government
wasn't till more than a month later
on September nine

melamine is good to add
to watery milk
because its cyanamides have the analytical characteristics of protein
molecules
you can use it to bulk up the apparent quality of your units
best of all
with its relatively low toxicity
melamine won't really hurt anyone
you can put it in a lot of things i mean
the only way you'd get bad effects would be if that was the sole food you
ate for say
six months
and who would do that?

'And leaned my head. I, too, had praise for your book ...'

i thought that visit would be
like the others
with us speaking to the students' politeness
but after a long train ride and a tiring walk
we three arrive on a busy street
meet your professor friend and his graduates
get led upstairs to a restaurant
where staff keep the hot dishes coming
and one by one we dine on our poems
could that happen where i come from? sweet potato in coconut cream
a regional speciality
a round table
the talk informal
each voice in turn
and in translation
but when you read
i question your ending
which tells of a woman embracing
her own silence
to become her lover's inspiration
can such listening be cause for celebration?

the work penetrates
                        me line
                        by line
but reaching its
irresistible conclusion
i pull back

since where i come from
one artist
among the many
we've belatedly learnt to appreciate

in the last few months of his life
was fêted

while beside him his helpmeet
through all of his struggles
who had given up her own work to do it
was obliged to spend his valedictory
looking at her shoe

perhaps she thought
that her work
could never be as good as his

i know we have to take responsibility if we choose to give up on our talents
but who would have raised their children if she hadn't? he was an alcoholic

your ballad lays bare just such traumatic dislocations
i ask
if in contrast to its final transcendent moments
it might be closed on a questioning note

why must the beloved fly to pieces
in the music incarnated by her silence?

at the end of the occasion
still talking
we walk mosaic streets to the station
call at a back-alley temple
braced in dark wood beams
get on the train

during the journey home you tell us
the restaurant was so noisy it was
hard to hear it's made your head ache
and then you retreat to a distant seat
what can i do?
i give you two of my Panadol

and from that moment my happiness about the day
leaks away
night descends
with my misgivings
i shared my reservations
so publicly
can you forgive me?
next morning guilty
i can't bear our polite exchange outside Pacific Coffee
what a coward not to discuss this with you directly
but would you let me?
perhaps you will speak with me again if i apologise in writing
i email
then you come and tell me not to worry i haven't offended you at all
and you say it with such a look of consternation
it makes me question my perception

but after that things won't come quite right between us
it's as if a light switch
develops an intermittent cut off

as if you encouraged me to be fearless
to accompany you to the cliff-edge view

and when i do
away you flew

swooping down from the clouds

it's like the establishing shot
from *Stargate Atlantis*
but architecturally more adventurous
speeding in from the airport
spring-clip bridges hook together a plait of land
loaded with building toggles
and we've just been introduced
your book about to be published in sixteen countries
all i know about your home is that during the 1999 APEC conference
three limousines with darkened windows slid past my gate
to open a reserve for José Rizal ten minutes' walk away at the end of my
    street
this morning i went to look again at this memorial on land reclaimed
beside Te Whau creek
someone has placed a wreath against the stone
it's just before New Year
perhaps it's there to commemorate the day of Rizal's execution
30 December 1896
my partner took a photo of me reading the engraving
so i'll send it to you
then i saw on a website about Rizal's final hours
his last poem
retrieved by his sister
from where he had hidden it in the gas stove in his cell
it farewelled both his country
and 'my sweet foreigner' the Irish woman
Josephine Bracken
who after her lover's judicial murder
spent some time nursing the men
hurt in the revolutionary struggle to oust the Spanish colonial
    administration
then later as the US took over
she chose to return to Hong Kong
the place she was born where she now married and gave birth to her
    daughter

but when they built the Happy Valley racetrack
her grave was obliterated
my garden backs on to a racetrack
which they are planning to redevelop as a housing and shopping precinct
on the website they also said that US governor Howard Taft
recommended José Rizal as a suitable figurehead
for national veneration
because his limited political agenda wouldn't flagrantly remind everyone
that rather than having sovereign independence
the Philippines were subject to military occupation by the US
under the previous Spanish regime
Rizal had got as far as advocating universal equality before the law
and education for all
Confucius famously approved of the latter
though by the way none for women
and further on line
i also read that the US administration
particularly liked Rizal for his education
stance
because a political focus
on teaching
implies
that while you have undeniable potential
you're not quite ready to manage as an independent adult
or vote

they say Rizal was shot because *Noli Me Tángere*
his hugely influential novel
was an affront to the Catholic hierarchy and its political clients

later you lent me a book called *The Library at Night* by Alberto Manguel
which catalogues among other things
book burnings through history
and how Christian missionaries
systematically
extinguished the Aztec libraries

stock in trade

1. because it's in your own language i find this one you've given me
 unreadable
but from who you are i know it is front-to-back sovereignty discourse
and i look at the photographs in it of your maternal ancestors and mentors

2. yours came winging in from the coast to be handed out the ranch sliders
 of condos
with Tia Marias mangroves big surf the seasons anatomised
and for the women characters a slow burning dissatisfaction with their
 bodies

3. with unassuming grace on our way somewhere else you hand me your
 text
i'd already absorbed its snowy breasts and desolate vaginas
its stick shifts and late night pick-ups on blind corners

4. i don't have a copy
but i've seen your 'pack shot'
what do i learn from it? keep mentioning the title if you want them to buy it

5. you read
it's a yeast extract
women's desire makes good activator

6. when i opened it
your book sang all over the room
then roosted in my brain until i caught it in a box and posted it home

7. written sold and prize winning
as yet unread by anyone
your annotated manuscript donated to the university's collection

8. i give my book to all of you
and as if that's who i am
you give me yours in return

some notes on shopping and present giving

our guide and comforter says 'what you need for Shandong
is long john underwear
and go to Sha Tin and buy a puffy coat in the sale at Yata'
so i do
it's monumentally crowded
but they have my size
enormous
i try it on among the security guards
marshalling shoppers and the frantic women
unpacking cartons of garments from The Mainland
i don't know if it's a bargain
and later one of us
who's a fashion voyeur
looks it over: 'wait
this outdoor gear you have on
is not
from New Zealand!'
as if i've committed a cultural faux pas
but when i shopped at home
for presents to bring
i went round the back streets of New Lynn
five minutes away from my address by car
that's my outdoors
casing the semi-industrial wilderness for souvenirs
but really what was there
in my price range that you can't get here or anywhere?
greenish stone and glass ornaments of wetas
Lord of the Rings rings
are these 'New Zealand'? iconic tea-towels
woolly animals and abalone fragments
all of it labelled 'from' here in that sneaky way
they have
to let the buyer know
it was actually manufactured
off shore

well what attracts me most
is a kiwi illustration
that i assume
was drawn by the artist Sydney Parkinson
on Cook's voyage of English annexation
but when i went back to check on his name
the shop had morphed into an internet café
and i couldn't track that bird reproduced in the resin disc
which purported to be sourced from the South Island
i expect you could've used a set of them as drink coasters
or chucked a couple into a kid's toy box
deposited them as windowsill knick-knacks
and when she saw me stroking one
the assistant had touted a 10 per cent discount
but i needed more than a solitary bird
fourteen to be on the safe side
and even with her reduction
they cost way beyond
what i could fund
though later when i got to this foreign destination
and was carrying out my present plan
i wished i'd bought a whole damned flock of them
because then nobody could have suspected me
of investing any personal feelings
in what i was offering
and if only i'd bought them
let that be a lesson
on the other side of the world
it is too late to procure some common old thing
from home
pāua cufflinks and woollen bonnets
steel axes to knock their socks off
and even supposing i did have time to send for such items
the air freight alone
would cost an arm and a leg
anyway despite these omissions
it all turned out for the best

because i had to go ahead with the awkward gifts
for which i'd opted
and to keep down the weight in my suitcase
what they were
was exactly the right number of cards
from a print over-run
that the artist Stanley Palmer gave me after an exhibition
called *Fragments and Reflections:*
Northland 1990
although i bet he's forgotten
and i've been sending them out one by one
to various people on many occasions
ever since
actually his images are so moody and existentially drear
they do for birthdays and sympathy
and with an up-beat handwritten note
also for Christmas and A Happy New Year
but in this foreign context
i relied on them to say: thank you so very much
i've come from somewhere rather dark and beautiful
far
far away from here
originally
there were five views from which to choose
but i've run out of the one which had the face of a Māori girl
foregrounding some sort of bleak rural backdrop
i used those up first
they must have spoken to me the most
but actually
she wouldn't have been any good for souvenir purposes
because in travel situations
i have a horror of unauthorised cultural appropriation
keep it inexplicit
and resin kiwis could be embarrassing too
since we have to admit that sooner or later
in all probability they'll be as extinct as the moa
thankfully the other Stanley Palmer images i had

were of unpeopled landscapes
with the seabed and foreshore
portrayed as somewhat tidied over
by European agriculture
but brooding skies and unforgiving hills
loom ominously into the picture spaces
remembering
these are only small reproductions
just standard post
nothing ostentatious about them
size wise
so what i thought was i would take enough
up here
for everyone i ought to give to
and then i'd go to the local equivalent of the two-dollar shop
and buy a heap of cheap frames
put them in
and offer the cards
like actual little Stanley Palmers
i knew i'd be able to get the frames cheap
because the two-dollar shopping village
where i live in Avondale
is full of them
so closer to point of origin i assumed
they'd cost peanuts
but actually
when i converted it
they wanted an equivalent
which means the cost of shipping halfway across the earth
is discounted
how do they work that out to make a profit?
or was the price in Hong Kong
inflated for bargaining? don't ask
i have an entrepreneurial bypass
even so the first thing i did on arrival was ferret out a shop
that had these little bits of equipment i needed
to enhance my cards' artistic status

and the outing i undertook
to do this
was to the mall fifteen minutes away on foot
from the place where i was staying
and i have to tell you that for over a week
i really needed help from my map
to get there or anywhere
actually even after a month
nothing much about the navigable geography of this place
sticks in my head
that's despite the fact that our hosts have walked us all over the
neighbourhood
several times
can you believe that? why am i so crap at directions?
is it something to do with lack of oestrogen? or what?
i can stand up and read to an audience
of five hundred people in a foreign city no sweat
but if you expect me to find my way to the venue unaided
i will have a panic attack
so from my point of view
just to get to the Jusco shopping centre was a triumph
if you want to know it's at Lok Fu MTR station
and go up to the top floor
where there are a few varnished benches in the foyer
elderly people from the neighbourhood like to sit there
which is not at all usual
since in this place most sitting-down-for-a-rest spots
are all about paying to go into some kind of restaurant
but here they were free
and i collapsed on those benches a few times
although i eventually felt intimations from seventy-plus passers-by
left standing
that benches aren't put outside the nothing-over-ten-HK-dollars shop
for tourists to flop on
in which case i assure you i would get up smartly and defer to my elders
even if my back did hurt
and then

when i had got my breath
i went in and chose and paid for fourteen plastic frames
not shiny ones
they were like Bakelite
kind of dull and unassuming
at first glance an affinity they had with the pictures themselves
but ultimately harmonising
as i happily found when i got them back to my room
and made one up as a sample
i didn't want anyone to catch me at this either
behind my locked door i felt like a forger
i had first to pull apart the purchased mounts
and it was then
with thirteen more ahead of me to assemble
that i understood all the human handiwork
that goes into these little mass-produced contraptions
a woman at some factory on The Mainland
had unmoulded the plastic surround
cut and placed the glass to fit it
added a light slice of paper
taped behind it a mini squab of shock-absorbing foam
then fitted over this a piece of hardboard with a hook she'd riveted in at the
top
and had also glued on a collapsible prop
to make the picture stand up
if that's what you want
and at each corner she had further screwed in
a pivoting flange
to lock in the backing
doubtless she'd done thousands an hour
my part of that
a fragment
wherein i centred my Stanley Palmer card face down on the glass
equidistant from the edges
fiddled the paper surround and framing foam
over the heart of this menagerie
then came the moment to insert the backboard

without upsetting the picture's symmetry
after which i could only hope
that when i flipped the whole lot upright
it would look spectacular
and i was not disappointed
not overly spectacular however
because i still had to be able to maintain
that though the value of the picture was intangible
which is the beauty of art for you
its price was demonstrably negligible
so when i presented it they'd know
it hadn't caused me any trouble
and i could take a that's-a-ten-HK-dollar-frame-around-a-card-i-had-at-home tone
but to establish that devil may care
i also had to decide about the packaging
which was another whole different ball game
but i had the most amazing luck
i had got
in the same cheap shop
a cellophane pack of fifteen paper bags in four pastel shades
each with a contrast strip of multi-coloured raffia plastic
to tie up the necks of the presents
maybe only a woman will understand what a coup that was
for instance
i have had many conversations with my mother
she's alive when i write this
about finding the correct gifts
and their appropriate accoutrements
so i know at least two of us are on the same wavelength
and also
when i went shopping at Walmart on The Mainland
with the visiting writers' liaison team
who were buying gifts for their colleagues back at the office
so they would know that even at a distance they were held in high esteem
and i suggested jasmine tea
they bought some for me

you do have to be so very careful what you say round present buyers
and you must never let them see you touch anything
in case they think you're hinting
but i'm not really sure about selecting for men
and i did wonder if any of them would be offended
if their gift came in a pink pastel packet
so i tried to be gender sensitive about it
although i think most male writers
are somewhat in touch with their feminine aspect
not Norman Mailer
but several of my girlfriends will understand why
that night
i found it hard to sleep
thinking how well my present assembling had worked out
but suddenly there came creeping over me
a terrible anxiety
because now although each gift was ready
it started to be hard to decide about the right way to offer them
several of the people were about to go home
on different days
those were my approaching deadlines
and if i mucked up the timing
how would i dispose of any ungiven pictures?
too awkward to pack them home my case was stuffed
would i have to abandon some? but on the other hand
i didn't want to distribute my gifts all at once
the thought of lugging them into an event in a clanking bag
gave me the heebie-jeebies
i was determined to give my gifts discreetly
because you can't help but notice the way people here
make everything a photo opportunity
but i wanted to give them as if they came direct from Aotearoa New Zealand
with me acting only as the intermediary
is that too weird?
which meant that since untying presents prolongs the suspense
there could be no bows

and even though the packages looked hugely pretty
all tied up
i decided i had to cut the raffia fastenings off
and let the pictures out
then how bad is this:
i worried that May
who'd been taking my towels away
and emptying the bin every day
but i never let her do any other cleaning
except for the sheets once a week
but i stripped the bed
oh all right i only know her name because on the last day
of my month's stay
she asked me to fill out her customer satisfaction card
and in all the option boxes on it i ticked excellent
exceeded expectations
which i would have done for any one of the nameless staff who'd been in
and seen my heap of framed scenes
in the wardrobe
and then in the fancy wrappings
so they knew my plans
and would think i was an idiot
when they saw all the snipped-up festive ties
in the rubbish
and would think i didn't have the courage of my convictions
but that's ridiculous
worrying about what other people think
though to be on the safe side
when i'd scissored them off
i buried the cut-up bits of ribbon in the bin
in an opaque plastic bag under some banana skins
and you see then when i gave the pictures
somewhat clandestinely
to each person
they could look straight into the plain pastel package
of gender-neutral colour
pull forth their picture

check it out
and put it straight back
so no one else even had to know or discuss what they'd got
and anyway if they did they wouldn't be disappointed
because all the pictures were the same
but different
in the sense that there were two separate views
but of equally moody landscapes
which is the way you give so there won't be any trouble among siblings
but then two of the recipients separately said 'did you paint this?'
i replied: 'i wish'
and one of them laughed and repeated it 'i wish' as if that was a piece of
    idiom unfamiliar to him
which made me feel clever again
but in a non-painterly way
only then i felt even more like a counterfeiter
since i didn't invent that riposte i got it off television
and i won't tell you how relieved i was
when all the pictures had been hand-delivered
but in the end i only gave out thirteen and kept one for myself
because i really like the way Stanley Palmer's images look
in the little Bakelite frames
and the one i kept is *Bay Harataonga – beyond Motutere – Floating Island*
when i look at it i'm reminded how anxious i get
yet things can still turn out
all right
when i got home
it was just before Christmas
and so then i went around finding individual presents
for a few more of the people i'd met up there
because it was a way of keeping hold of them
and not
quite
being back here
for good
yet
because it was The Festive Season

i didn't have to worry that anyone would take these gifts personally
although this time
that's secretly how i intended them
and after my agonies over the generic presents
i hope you can understand
that deciding what to give
and then sending the right specific stuff
to each recipient
was quite an undertaking
which i won't go into here
because it's too excruciating

a writing exercise

1. in these hours i meet the translation students
and give them a creative writing exercise
which is to record in detail
everything they remember seeing
through an important window in their lives
not fiction i tell them
write only the facts
this is an entirely factual task
but if there is anything out there
about which you think we should know more
invent it
the whole to be completed in such a way
as to make this external view
a self-portrait

afterward their professor tells me he sees this task
as a metaphor
of how a piece of work from one language
gets translated into another

2. then a student at the Mainland recital
asked why i don't use much in the way of punctuation or capitals
was i affected by e.e. cummings? and what made me take up a career as a
    poet
when she put her questions it was well past the finish of my performance
i had left the stage and was sitting in the audience
hearing my name mentioned i twisted around in my seat to pay attention
but the things she wanted to know seemed to go on for such a long time
that when i got to my feet and faced the packed room
i felt so astonished to be questioned about such matters
i forgot what she'd asked and had to get her to repeat herself
which she did
word for word

3. yes e.e. cummings affected me
i remember in the fifth form reading 'Buffalo Bill 's defunct'
and identifying wildly
with the lack of capitalism
and since the poem said Buffalo Bill was finished
that also suggested it could be the right moment for Annie Get Your Pen
and what i want to know is how do you like your hazel-eyed girl Mistress
    Birth?
but according to an article i read later in the *New Yorker*
using lower case marks me as a perennial teenager
and i see from her Grattan Prize judge's notes that Fleur Adcock isn't
    fussed on it either
grounds for instant dismissal
that *New Yorker* writer said something like e.e. cummings' distinctive style
equates with the 'cool' kid in dark glasses determined to attract our stares
without letting us see his eyes
a look-at-me display which i would add
has a particular jurisdiction
in the phallic-feminine
since however longingly we gaze at her
she is bound not to let us in there
sluts show up in the spotlight
to escape contempt a good woman needs protective gods or power suits
preferably both
without them
i've adopted
in
visibility
to carry my lower case into middle age
but i'm no teenager
and as i said this
i looked around and saw i was the oldest woman in the room
was it my imagination? or did those young Mainlanders
seeing my body
experience a shudder of horror

4. so apart from looks
at my age
i require another reason
to carry on the lower-case first person
which is that for me it represents
ideographically
the interrupted narratives of women's lives
menstruation domestic celebration
rape pregnancy abortion
child birth and breast feeding
story telling
getting the shopping and doing the cleaning
keeping the fire and finding dinner
not omitting any of those private & public tasks and rituals
which must be accomplished before anything else is
even when beside ourselves
and from our mothers we inherit this mantra: me~no~pause
but now my daughters
are interrupting: 'you never do any bloody cleaning'
please
excuse me for a moment
while we settle a family disagreement

5. whereas
to my mind
the upper-case first person
reads as the default generic setting
of uninterrupted male subjectivity
as neutral and universal in patriarchy
in relation to which
a woman artist
must perpetually distinguish herself

and since my reading of Bracha Ettinger
the lower-case first person
also speaks to me
of self-fragilisation
in any body

6. why did i choose a career as a poet?
career? that implies financial reward
i have been paid in many jobs
but practically speaking
despite spending the best part of my adult life writing
money comes to me from poetry only intermittently
and being invited to a writers' workshop
is like winning the lottery
so even though here i am wearing a 'poet' label
the moment your backs are turned
it washes off
at present it is my partner far away on the other side of the world
who supports me
then i lifted up my arms and said: 'thanks be to him'

7. why poems?
because the novel is harder
takes years longer
and apart from the Jane Austens among us
who can fit writing one in
around all the other things? i take my hat off
to these novelists
whereas if i get the gist of it noted
i can keep a poem to finish later
and once i sit down and start typing
i'll look up after what seems like five minutes
to find that several hours have passed in the space of a heartbeat
which means this work goes on
aside from time
i like that
into a world of busynesse
my poems come
between the dot and the stroke

8. then i decided this piece was complete
so i got up from my screen
and seeing the dishes

took a walk on the racecourse
where i remembered something else
how after i spoke
you stood and talked in another one of those languages i haven't learnt
beside me
there came a murmur 'he's saying
good things about you'
but what were they? i'll never know
then we all went back onstage for the official photo
and when it was over five students mobbed me
for individual shots
and autographs
standing on the podium with them i thought
this is too conspicuous
what about the men? i better get off
but until those girls
                                        and one boy
were finished
i didn't

仁

'ren' is
literally
the sign for man
and the number two
today some agree to translate it as co-humanity
and as far as that goes
i do
but here it is
stripped back
to the pre-Confucian etymology

仁
the distinctive quality of a man
manliness

connotes among other things: gentility softness
graceful complaisant mildness

lenity
comity
temerity

mansuetude
forbearance

patient and tender
tolerant yielding
to my mind aspects of a person
preparing to open

仁
look at him
projections from and into his person
what he gives and receives

in intellectual consciousness
and from an erect penis

when they write rape scenes
with women in them
replace all the feminine with masculine pronouns

and 仁
as you rock in *the morning blue*
know that 'goddess of evil'
is the queen in you

on the first day

they put us out at the confluence of three streets
that once were creeks
stunned we look up
at the *Titanic*s of Patriarchal Capitalism
someone has a camera
but it's like when you're part of the fault
trying to capture the heft of an earthquake
the light is pearled grey with poisons
overcome by the weight of the buildings
we can't shop
among the inhabitants
these louring floors are bulwarks
they are tracts
but not built bigger for my pleasure
i rely on the clitoris
where the nerves are
little to speak of in the vagina
birth pain
arises from the uterus
now a woman collecting rubbish
comes across
and pats my back
i don't understand what she says
but her gestures approve of my carrying a supermarket recycle bag
she pushes a trolley stacked with flattened cartons held on with bungy
cord
hair wrapped in a scarf
hands protected in canvas gloves
someone else directs me onto the correct bus
and spends the journey sat beside me
moaning about her heartless brothers
every Sunday she takes their mother a cooked meal
she makes herself
and shows me in her basket a tier of canisters
rice above vegetables above chicken and dumplings

i despair of my brothers they don't visit Mum they give her nothing she
says
opposite us
in its stroller
a drowsy toddler's head
sags forward
as its caregiver lowers the back rest
it wakes
and cries
so she leans close
and drums on its chest
in a heartbeat
returns it to sleep

Nan Lian Garden

Diamond Hill where taxis swash
in and out the all-day dusk
under the motorway ribs

clomp the road to The Buddhist Pine no climbing
high hawk harrying
no video

a stringed instrument on continuous playback
tings
against the traffic

along the myrtle path plastic
other cans mondo grass tall as my hand
the architecture pavilion's scaled model of a man

in agony his back carries the pole and truss bracket
holds up a roof
lips wrenched horizontal one visible tooth

birds rustle the common crepe myrtle
every two hours the outdoor marble table is
disinfected

bus rush on the overpass
banyan grove Golden Temple
but why didn't Jesus of Nazareth appoint any women disciples?

kneeling
the three women gardeners have plastic buckets
beneath their straw hats they are faceless mechanical weed handlers

striated rock
in its crack
leaf flourishes

information kiosk
under maintenance
dragon pot pompom twist bougainvillaeas

Dad said if bougainvillaea gets away it'll pull down your house
he was wrong about so much
these ones tamed to within an inch of their trunks

vermilion bridge closed
pool lilies pinked
on heart-shape leaves

Nan Lian Hall temporarily closed
across the barrier through colonnades of wooden pillars
beats the dark entrance

elm hill fragrance hill holly path
green arbour wooden seat
sore back massage a hand-size bird flushed from the branches

shadows of trees in which i fold away my pointy sunglasses
found at the charity sale: for elders
we don't want anything left to pack Dear buy them it's in a good cause

with their amber tints perched on my nose i am a witch
a week today i'll take up my cloud pine branch
and fly into the Mainland winter

feeling the cold
yet receiving sparks
witches go lightly clad

these frames the precise colour of my 'beautiful
hat': that's what you said
jointy nose upstaged by my clothes

ting music wound
in this pylon vista between skyscrapers
broad scarf thrown around my shoulders wraps down these chest
vibrations

man up a three-legged ladder
clipping
waterwheel draws deep poem traffic humming

look again through the bridge gate at The Golden Temple
its wooden roof washed with light
reflect on The Prophet Mohammed's revelation of the sensual fruits of
paradise

but which translation? Arabic: dark-eyed maidens
or Syriac: white raisins – of crystal clarity
my hesitancies

grey carp adrift
a trickle bed of stones
deep pool – amber splash

green niche plants on the wheel house
fat free-standing bauhinia at the water's edge
not the national tree our guide said carefully: symbol of Hong Kong only

in its trunk
knot eyes opening
look at me

to Long Men Lou Restaurant: feasters hurrying
behind the waterfall people digging
chopsticks in vegetarian

bowl laden waiters
souvenir shop
when our Mainland trip is finished you demand to know what i got

my counter attack: 'what did you get?' 'nothing'
then i confess
to four woven basket fridge magnets

your 'English Class':
'Does Jane pay enough?'
'Yes, but not much.'

get the goods home
where one reed-and-willow-coloured plaster-of-Paris replica is dropped
its beautiful handle falls off

whatchamacallit women's art
does get knocked about
handle-less i clamp it to the fridge with the others

understand the 'tragic' characters of male authors
the Emma Bovarys and Anna Kareninas
not suicides: murders

aching back
in the rock garden big cold stone
i want

on top a turtle shell where crested finches bathe and sparrows drink
to Chi Lin Nunnery: exit only
that won't do me

little kids
running in
shushed down by blue-shirt guard's outstretched hand shuddering at them

solidified crackle mud
spider-web rock
don't touch! water shoots mist the milk boulders

lotus pond
dry hill traffic
humming apartments

no idea what's here until i breach the curtain wall
and find this whole garden i walk in
is the province of The Abbess

three gates: wisdom compassion and the skilful means
which are
faith understanding and practising the important paths to liberation

imposing courtyard
Golden Buddha
but why did The Fourteenth Dalai Lama say homosexuality is
misbehaviour?

don't sit in here closed to visitors
chanting off key and back in tune
crossing the vermilion bridge the washerwoman showers me with kisses

taken
slowly
amber delicious

light
felt more strongly
through thinner layers

tea pavilion
green hill behind the lotus pool
swoop of rooves

raincloud rock
sun jabber
fluent tongue

pee Panadol German on cellphone
photo opportunity: walk down
through the car canyon and out of the dark

glasses on
i'll come again
borne here more times with other people

‘What is it makes the stranger?’

hailing across the house of song
the house of the family
tax house   garden house   the house of desire   the house of sleep
frozen bullets of oxygen weed
a handful of these clouded beads
knit in a small garment for my heart to beat against your absence
its blank grafted skin

one
another
the way you talk
sometimes to people who won’t listen
who gently move to be further from your voice its insistence
but i who want to know what you said
cannot cross the language torrent

if i take these links
could there be enough? for a bridge of words
a clash of swords
the ocean strand from a window you’ve opened
escaping captivity
making the fire exit

beads bought at The Ladies’ Market
stretched apart
then sprung together
given my daughters
thirteen to a circlet

no longer belonging to me
they grow cold and heavy

that blackbird
still in the grass
is it? there

look away
let culture take its course

but i am sure i do not want your teachers' praise: 'wonderful' 'marvellous'
answer me this:
what puts out a fire? tearing a tender crust for the sweet dark meat of
desire

– rain
introduces me to the earth

women's work

interference

the disturbing effect of new learning
on the performance of behaviour previously learned, with which it is inconsistent

1. you are not the only one in this hotel in this city of so many
who are alive in their beds
but perhaps only you would mention it walking out of the lift

2. when sex happens among us some men treat women as if we are voiceless
are they deaf?

3. most ways most times
i am in my lover's hand
a sack of grain s!he
lifts the light
out of me
a consequence of happiness

4. on days of sorrow we may say
Dad listen: i couldn't help carry you out of the church the past weighs too much
or
only yours? was i not meant to do my own work?

5. we'd like to get completely out of it
but with all that pōrangi in the family
rarely have the luxury

6. someone else says quarantine the bitch
why not? so i have my work cut out
and piece together my vanity of human wishes
with fear of the authorities
expatronising ladyfingers shovelover narcissistic coloniser
all of the above

copping to it
poetessentialism womanipulative
words to choke on
but my worst crime is aspiration above my station

7. do you ever have time to think of such matters? is it permitted?
or shall you adopt the authoritative tone
and go on
march all over
unless exercising your prerogative
not to
and when you do so choose
for some reason
i only seem able
intermittently
to be grateful

8. but what you've said
i read
and raised my head

walking the dark hall

1. above his picture in the hotel stairwell
she asks what i think
of him? ab*so*lute power
corrupts ab*so*lute*ly

she chastises me
everything
he did for The People

2. at the shrine
three People's Army soldiers
climb on each other's shoulders
balance
on a ledge
for a daredevil photograph
watching them
she says
to dig the children out
after the earthquake
our soldiers made a superhuman effort

3. graduation bears
everywhere
cameras snap
swollen letters snake into certificates

4. at the years-after party
bystander to their grand passion
i search out my old flatmate
confess how i've envied a love like that
she sets down her drink
envied a hole in the head she said

5. the mothers' worry
why are our children crying as they swallow?

the nurses administering the poison reassure them:
he says it is a temporary bitterness before we meet in paradise

6. so far i've been spared ever meeting a single soul to overrule my better
 judgement
though here
i know
i have
had my head
turned
but thanks be to the God i don't believe in we aren't the people in our
 poems

7. that is The People's Army Barracks
voices subdued as we pass it

8. Father Peter Murnane
Adrian Leason and Sam Land
are on trial in Aotearoa New Zealand
for deflating the pure white bubble cover of the Waihopai listening station
now on TV we can see there is a swivel dish beneath the collapsed plastic
the Government didn't want anyone to know where the American
 intelligence was pointing
it was
too sensitive

the accused say the authorities direct Waihopai
to find out what people think
and arrest them for it

the jury deliberate for two hours
and acquit

9. why do they want to enlist me in this dispute about the gondola?
we'll ride to the mountain top! she is unswervingly in favour
you say: 'ab*so*lute*ly not!'
since yous ask me to decide

i say majority rules let's vote on it
how you laugh at that
unwitting political theatre
then somehow
we all wind up here
together

10. descending
our cabin swings off the cliff face
misty pens write and rewrite the horizon
holding hands
up we stand
you tell us to sit down
yes i know   below us in the snow   pointed reasons

of our lucky eight

1. only seven writers came
when we left for The Mainland
because our compatriot was adamant he would not abandon his spouse
in a foreign city
but i thought he should
because Hong Kong doesn't seem that foreign to me
though i know after these cocooned weeks
i might be kidding myself

2. then at the airport the Hawaiian fell out
and flew home to North America
because he had not arranged a multiple-entry visa
before he left he told me to look out over there
for a solid gold panda
and buy it
since precious metals are appreciating
which means the value of pure metal objets d'art is skyrocketing
he was right but i didn't see any
and it's hard to understand why someone with such forward-looking
entrepreneurial thinking
didn't complete the multiple-entry visa requirements they'd dinned into us
perhaps he expected an exception for him?
The Mainland may be Hong Kong's first cousin
but at the border they treat each other like freeloading relations
or was he just homesick for his woman? and longing to cook that bird he
    had
stowed in the freezer for a belated Thanksgiving
several times
as the day loomed closer
he mused to me about making us a Turkey Dinner
with all the requisite trimmings of harmony and gratification
and even priced a big one
at Jusco
but with only a microwave and a printer in our communal room
roasting was

impossible
in New Zealand
because of the land thefts
typically
our day for celebrating national identity is rancorous
and since tangata whenua are determined to stop Pākehā pretending amnesia
nobody but a political activist of some sort would hurry home for it
according to this doctrine
until the Treaty of Waitangi is honoured
no fattened animal shall be forgiven
and every February sixth the only bird on our table is tino rangatiratanga gnaw on that

3. the rest of us can form a line at the departure gate
where i watch you get pat-down searched
arms hung out like an old shag
how humiliating this is
i look away
then it's my turn
and for the first time
in a kind of solidarity with you i too raise my arms
but with this acquiescence i've invoked the full treatment
knob on a bumpy X of arms and legs
head tilted watch the hands travelling unimpeded
and if she
or i
want in
i can't stop them
she does her worst
when i snap at her she looks across at her boss expressionless
he shrugs
we board our aircraft
in the seat beside mine i find the stranger
has been studying at an institution minutes up the highway from my home
he tells me how good his business is
and that he's off to see his relations

they're having a family conference since things in his marriage
aren't going so well
sitting the other side of him she smiles
does she know what he's saying? or could that smile be
her version
woman to woman
of his candid other-language revelation?
but perhaps he is taking advantage of the fact that in English
she has no idea what he's talking about
is that where their disharmony starts? and all the while the baby stands
alert
in front of us
on its maternal grandmother's lap
peeping over the seat
back
at its mum and dad

whenever my relations convene for one of these
familial disharmony conferences
i want to speed screaming over the horizon like this plane

4. only now there's an announcement
Jinan City is fogged in
we're coming down
i hear no grumbling
everyone buckles
are we so stoic? no
at home i think we'd growl
though who in their right mind
wants to be blown off a runway into the ocean?
much preferring a little intelligence rendition
to transit lounge purgatory
safe hands freezing to our luggage at Hefei
we descend the steps to the tarmac
lurch onto a bus in which an array of first-class passengers
let off before us
are holding themselves incommunicado across the rear seat

sturdy suits feet planted wide apart
ensuring that
they take up all the space they've paid more for
thigh pressing thigh so determined are they to keep every single one of us
economy-class travellers
on our feet
strap hanging our eyes register this phalanx of superior comfort and rise
above it
to the terminal
business
as usual

5.
in the transit lounge one of us begins to feel anxious about her conference
call
regarding the real estate development project
she's negotiating
on which she must speak with her partners every single evening
at eight
and then work on through the night
writing is her recreation
she doesn't need much sleep
while all the rest enter a vegetative state
and you pace the airport's carved soapstone sales outlets
she strategises her departure
warns us
she is about to cross over
from transit to the terminal proper
and once this separation is enacted
she will disappear from my life forever
there can be no communication between transit and onward departures
she will book a direct flight to Hong Kong
and then be off to her home in the US
so here let me remember the last things of her i have:
she is wearing palest mocha tartan cashmere separates
incorporating a red thread
her hair a sleek veil tied in a ponytail

and because the female border guards confiscated all her contact solution
glasses
also impounded was the Dior moisturising skin food in her make-up case
in many dozens of international flights this has never happened before
but of course she can't publicly voice her objections
i think those
border guard women
craved the cosmetic secrets of her honeyed complexion
and since all the checked baggage is still locked up
in the belly of the jet
she is also vindicated in taking on and off as hand luggage the other
possessions she has
in her little wheelie-case
and years and years of the unpredictability of Mainland travel
have taught her
not
to let it out of her sight
because if your stuff gets lost
which simply cannot be the fate of her business papers
Red Rover
project's over
but now she tosses her champagne down coat across her shoulders
and departs without further notice
she is a multi-lingual force of culture
freed from the city of smog

6. that leaves only four men
and me
in our writers' party
who will be next? when i intone this
the others look perplexed
but here we are
in an airport version of *The Blair Witch Project*
and guess what? i'm not so secretly elated
at having to face the literary wilds with a reducing coterie of talent
and thanks to these unexpected defections
from now on
perhaps those left will be forced to make more than polite conversation

it's like being in a parallel version of that Oriental Parade episode
where i was twenty-one
and lived with seven men
as a restorative after the Snow White Rose Red Nurses' Home
but here
including our leaders
the sex ratio is two femme to five of them
why should i care? because culture warns me everywhere
that in men's eyes
i've entered my invisible years
at fifty-plus i am an object of no significance
and when the others collect their luggage
one of their suitcases has also vanished
so yet another writer is left
waiting for his stuff as we bus off
but at our overnight destination he catches up with us
later explaining
he got sent to the wrong hotel
where he found he was 'expected to share a room
with the most beautiful woman on our plane'
who helped him check in
in Mandarin
but then the reception staff paired him with someone less thrilling
so he got in a taxi
and after some protracted driver misunderstandings
managed to direct it
to where we're staying
and rocks up

7. but really
in the scheme of dramatic narrative conflicts
could his plane woman help being both the most beautiful
and also unavailable?
would she sooner share a room with him? or me? i am a fearless traveller
    also
i've rafted the Mississippi with Huck and Jim
lazed in the spa with The Wife of Bath

argued with Lucy Honeychurch's cousin in Florence
galloped the tundra with Lyra Belacqua
and just for starters
sailed with Lady Barker
who after she crawled into a sunny corner
among the boxes of oranges
with which the deck was crowded
lay there helpless
and utterly miserable
but when our flight got bumped
she pulled herself together
and came along with me to Hefei
en route to Shandong
and in Hong Kong on the way home
we all sat together quite happily
in vacant sunlit airport spaces
waiting for our flight for hours
and these figments of my imagination weren't offended by my barely
    suppressed glee
when on one leg of our journey you had to buckle in beside me
they didn't stampede out of their seats
the moment the caution take off and landing lights were extinguished
to commandeer unoccupied space at the back of the cabin
in preference to being restrained for several hours
in the company of an excitable middle-aged woman
intent on deciphering their stylistic tics
and proposing they compose collaborative poems
while enquiring after the genesis of their magnum opuses
they were quite happy discussing religion and holidays and circumspect
    politics
with our minders and colleagues
slurping coffee and noodles
rewriting our futures

8. hmmmmmmm
on the other hand
your determined exit reminds me of that time
when going home on the railcar to Taranaki

i met Paul McCartney
and he sang to us unaccompanied between Marton and Hāwera
shouted fries and steak 'n' cheese pies at Taumarunui
– it was right before he met Linda Eastman and turned vegetarian
and as the train drew in to New Plymouth
my girlfriend and i attempted to introduce him to our waiting mothers
and fathers
but it was one a.m.
and quite understandably
tired from all the attention
preferring to remain incognito
he sped off along the platform
in the other direction
perhaps you're my middle-aged willed manifestation of him?
although
my Beatle was George Harrison
when i said so
Paul seemed a bit disgruntled
and later
you look askance
when i ask if you got any sleep back there
well hullo
i know why you left
just winding you up
but what a hopeful bugger it is
to watch you hold that animated conversation
in the baggage reclaim
with the charming young woman
from the couple you chatted to
for hours
on the plane
who you'll never
meet again

The Anthology of Women's Poetry

down a footpath running west off Peel Street
north of Hollywood Road
you bring
to the artists' hangout Club 71
named for its echoes of Tiananmen
an anthology you've edited with a friend
all the ways to be a femme
canvassed in eleven sections:
creator   family   archetype   explorer
keeper of memories   keeper of secrets
myth maker   freedom fighter
ageing   landscape   lover

i buy it
but why my disquiet? seeing this fat volume
is it disconcerting because i remember Riemke Ensing's 1977 *Private Gardens*?
anthology of New Zealand women's poems
from Trevor Reeves' Caveman Press
and recall how not much more than thirty years ago
such a collection's very existence was seen as problematic by some critics
or am i just miffed
because all of a sudden you expect me to fork out forty NZ dollars
and cheap at the price if i have it

we sit out on the walkway in warm electric light
the other side of the alley
nested in boxes
some cats alick
then two Pekingese arrive with a tableful of talkative women
and pointedly ignore the stray felines bristling
so feeling secure they settle back
alick

poems that merge the animal with the feminine
let us deconstruct them: i want to hear from any body pissed on

when i spoke of *Private Gardens*' reception to Riemke Ensing
i said: 'you know how it is
sometimes we want to diss our mothers'
'my mum and i' she replied
'are very close'
i take *Private Gardens* off my shelf
it's a withdrawn library copy
very ragged
from all the women who've read it
and now i've spent several happy hours ploughing through *Not A Muse*
and feel astonished
i too questioned the necessity for such a compilation
what's going on? it's as if without realising
i've somehow absorbed 'post-feminism'
and was attempting to swim with these men of The Mainstream

but just before i got caught in the current
a mate flung me an essay by Rachel Cusk
reprinted from the *Guardian* in the Melbourne *Age*
i must have forwarded it on to most of my writing friends
though some find its style impenetrable and academic
i like it

referencing Woolf and de Beauvoir
Lessing and Chekhov
in a nutshell Rachel Cusk says: men aren't expected to shed their gender
to be in the swim
so if they have their sexualities bobbing along with them
why shouldn't women? our sexuality is part of what makes us fully human

but the texts recognised most often as achieving literary distinction
have usually jettisoned what society determines as feminine
because in patriarchal cultures
those aspects of our identities are deemed inferior

whereas narratives that have a male protagonist
or with settings in which women are peripheral
are more likely to be praised as aesthetically reputable
while with a few notable exceptions material centred in the feminine
is treated as ephemeral

Rachel Cusk believes
that unlike the 'texts of change' she deems masculine
there's paltry recognition for what she calls 'the texts of repetition'
which inhabit the cyclical cultures of women

and Virginia Woolf's imperative
that women artists
must aspire to *A Room of One's Own*
is questioned too
Rachel thinks that to write out of communal and domestic spaces
enacts a discourse of the feminine
which strengthens our ability
to evade the dictates of patriarchy
and that option i would add
is equally open to men
but we women should get on with identifiably feminine writing
whatever
that
is

– and when i got home i shifted my screen
to *The Matrixial Borderspace* of the living room

banquet

1. it's the day after the banquet
to which i did not wear the finery i'd bought
a stretchy black waistcoat with a scoop neck

the only photograph i have of me dressed in it
seems the uniform choice of a car rental business
but i did come to my senses over the other garments

a cerise chiffon wrap coat
what was i thinking? it's just armholes in mosquito netting
and a black drape top through which one might strain junket

but despite my expensive preparations
i found no occasion for these fashions
they hang in the wardrobe unworn for the duration

before any occasion i look in there
and feel a frisson as if from vivid frescoes in a private catacomb
all the while realising they'll crumble in sunlight

i thought these festivities required raiment
but when i saw the male writers dressed so conservatively elegant
or in your case so roughly inconspicuous

i too wanted camouflage
to be a thrush in a bush a crayfish on her seafloor coastal migration
a cow in a thicket

but i did like the way my Velcro-fastened wallet could be
slung over my shoulder till my back hurt
and then made safe as a pouch at my waist

i liked my flour-bag linen smock buttoned to the neck or not
and my fluff of black cardigan with its little bits of pilling
spilling like the cinders in *Spirited Away*

i am pleased with my drab elastic-waist cotton pants
and the wide scarf i apply like a force-
field wrapper contains an infanta

but when i get home i donate my fancy
unworn garments
to the second-hand shop

i don't have the energy for fash-femme i can't be fucked
but don't forget
my pleasure

undressed in the secrecy of the hotel mirror
i saw flesh i saw living tissue and walked out
introduced myself to the landscape

2. most of the locals and expats i met
dress elite neat
though at the banquet you don't project that

being tall helps
you wear your je ne sais quoi in a velvet coat
and those glasses with dramatic frames are always a good sign

i find i can talk to you like we're on the same hammock
you'll be visiting New Zealand soon and so you can find my house
remember from the road it is ten steps

and two up to the door at the front
walking its wood floors
like balancing on a raft afloat

then as i traverse its hall at night
from waves of sleep out dark windows
a river of cars

but i never went to your apartment
and wonder how far off the ground it is in the silence of the sky
a family quiet beneath your feet

though here most people also have
to be quiet beneath the feet of others above
they say your place goes up to a roof terrace

when we were in the flower market
to adorn it you bought a red-berried Christmas bush
and in the restaurant while we ordered you lodged this rustic pot on the
    seat

then remember those dirty looks we got? from the proprietor's family
who were eating dinner round the table in the shop doorway
but as you shifted the pot to the floor the atmosphere abruptly cleared

we had that drink
and went to the after-hours club
at the hair salon where the room was packed with blues musicians

tunes to carry the emotional weight of the day
up the spiral staircase
and across the uneven surface of the mezzanine

where i trip up
and my solo expletive rackets round the walls
conspicuous

then called on
how will i entertain?
despite my assiduous attempt to memorise 'Tūtira Mai' before i came

at the critical moment no waiata offers its confidence
Ki-a k' tapa-tahi, Ki-a ko-tahi rā   trips me every time
think as one   act as one   dream on

instead i come up with some lame thing
in English: *how long? how long? has this been going on?*
i said how long? how long? baby how long?

our friend performs in Ryukyuan
we applaud him

you tender your melancholy to the occasion
and when we leave at one a.m.
remain

out there

singing

morning after: morning before

so as not
to sit staring at the walls
i'm prepared to wear anywhere on the MTR

how about the bird sanctuary?
reachable from the rail skeleton
running through the body of the city emptying into the wetland

quiet! birds have ears
the river twists through green below the hill on the horizon
turns a corner to the ocean

one side of the current some white long-necked bank dweller
this side the compact yellow-billed black feather
look from the curtain wall apartments for the Rising Eastern Marsh
    Harrier
birds are – flying into this poem
in border threads of roadside particulate i embroider them:

Common Buzzard   Common Kestrel
Spotted Dove   Red Whiskered Bulbul

i embroider them on a wrapper of imported dust storms
in carnelian strands of bird lungs i embroider them
Eurasian Tree Sparrow   Black Drongo   Crested Myna
among the tiers of rusted containers at Lau Fau Shan
in the herd of cows swaying up the road ahead of the bus
on our way back from the depleted fishing village
my stitches
on the street of uninhabited shacks kept as tourist picturesque
where ducks ducks ducks fly up
and i embroider them

Grey Heron
golden eyes creamy silk pinions

snow-tipped wings
these ones are teenagers
but will soon have more black plumage

and if you do recognise these squawks
you'll know they are my culture
not my nature

water and bank mudskipper
mud hole mouth gasps
its back has the crest
tail sinuous
and here are red-clawed crabs in slow-mo across the yellow slop
that scuttle into apertures
which are their curtain wall apartments

people tramp behind me on the boardwalk sways not suitable for strollers
mangrove associates
since they have passports
may grow elsewhere
mangrove exclusives are the really tough plants
which have to stay here
but these audiences won't tear me to pieces
for employing one of the most insidious colonising powers
English speakers aren't yet taken to task
though always the warning impulse
someone has put out a sign:
closed official mind deep water

vibrating to my eye ladybird
fly fly no entry
but this hide bubbles with Cantonese voices
and they are not intimidated

in the butterfly garden silk vest purple miniskirt knee-high boots
with a Wasp in goggle specs striped jeans and striped shirt

a pair of yellow butterflies sparring
black and white spots

dark plant stalks
above green water
jolts
below the leaves

flutterboy emerging
with away over there an old shack by the concrete strut bridge
someone's miserable dwelling
move on!
wake up!
at the heart of a misunderstanding what have we got?

    i am prepared to stroke the parchment
    my brush dab dabs the rim of the ink –

grasses tremble above their plip-plop green drink
taking the cobble path
wild side walk: big ant

uniformed guards chat in the shade
yellow fish jumps
'let the good times roll' t-shirt

    – but you won't write back

come to the point rock:
some things in our lives only happen in ourselves
from his one good eye the man on the bench looks up
applies his telescope
and why not?
i gaze in on the blind side to find what i most want

not far away
a butterfly

has no hard shell
it is easy for it to become prey
they struggle to survive
at different times
with different tactics
Common Mormon escapes predators' eyes because it resembles birds' faeces

Lemon Emigrant
Mottled Emigrant
Grass Demon

a smell of denial
gestures of erasure
here is a wasp insect – don't be afraid
say it:
grass-flowers pink feathered candles rise through deeper orange starbursts

butterfly paddling pool
crimson and green   Cinnamon Batavia   birds cheeping work in progress
no entrance
what doesn't smell delicious?
Hitachi Lady

thigh-high bush fragrance
wild coffee

rubber ring saviour *Psychotria asiatica*
slow flow insects
snail
cockabully: sentence him to prison   wash hands immediately

shadow dragon fly: let him land
saffron thread legs vibrate   white tissue pond flowers above green leaf plate
three silver handbasins   white crocuses blow up

sanitise
if you touch
any   bird   thing

a feather
a petal

yellow greasy globe flowers growing above water   sex doesn't get any
    easier
the wet lands stretch into the distance
enter them

and what were the chances? in a city of millions
that i would run into someone i know

after a couple of hours
i encounter you two women
who tell me about 'yuánfèn'
meeting the person
when you most need them
so
we three get in a taxi
and go

have lunch at an Indian restaurant
where one of us worries
that the proprietor seeing her
will recall her spouse
since divorced
unhappy happy times and powerful men must be recovered from

is it any consolation? that: 'in my father's house are many mansions'
well perhaps
but mostly in terms of the matrimonial property act
Jane Austen knew all about that
no i can't keep my mouth shut
Blake was right 'the tigers of wrath are wiser than the horses of instruction'
so why

despite my deep scepticism regarding the astrological symmetries we share
do i still go and gaze at the horse fridge magnet i bought there?

it has smiling chops
it has legs that fly every which way against a red sky
and a small copper cloud attached to its fetlocks

wisdom
is for old women
and some women
rinse their hair
mine's white
where it isn't iron stripes
cut short
you're still in there
but here's something more of which it would be good to be aware:
snake traces have recently been found in the flower beds of this park
please for your own safety do not go into them
or the shrubberies
without permission

if any trace of a snake is spotted
do not attempt to catch it
stay
calm
and immediately inform our park staff
Leisure Cultural Services thank you for your co-operation

the path we're on is asphalted up to its green-banked margin
but if you wish there are many places to slip into this bush you'd call forest

where we'll be equally lost
though for someone staying in
is that a problem?

and if you sense the approach of The Ur-Serpent
undo

yourself
read her lips
read ink in the feminine
she's spelt in your hand
save her

*

101 snapshots

> *Small idle ghosts I had written,*
> *forgotten, never since seen,*
> *Slip into my brain; say, 'We were part of you'*
> – Robin Hyde

1

trampoline
the stepchild's
sitting room

2

the quarry two cars
eight men
five hours

3

starlight reserve
night fell in
my lap

4

grown-up children
shut bedroom doors
who is in there?

5

the disused warehouse burns
don't be cynical about love
seventeen fire engines wet it down

6

a beautiful man
i forget my order
a beautiful woman i forget my change

7
i wash my friend in sunlight
and moonlight
who will die first?

8
in my dream
your arm came under my breast
and held me warm and light like the scarf i bought myself

9
since long before
i've written about tea
but i was never so thirsty

10
i found this pure gold chain broken on the forecourt at the service station
mine i'd pressed on the wife at the pensione
because her husband expected something for nothing

11
Aunt's plants are hungry in the pot
she lived in her garden
which one is she? asks the gardener

12
privately the groom advises:
girls don't sit with their legs apart
i am to be her maid of honour

13
fog driving
heart talk
moon opens up on the bypass

14
one photograph shows crumbs on the keyboard
cat delete restore swoons purring in my arms
what does a girl have to do to get a cup of dry pellets around here?

15

listen!
that's a hungry cry
turn up the music

16

a Māori woman in a burqa asks me for directions
i can't help her
but suggest she check the address with the nuns

17

in bomber heaven
to make a good impression
you need a government contract

18

in porn king heaven
he has the remote control
but they don't know

19

i wanted to write something for the earth
but she turned green and started throwing up
so i left it

20

we have that cup of coffee
my heart set
call an ambulance

21

leaves left up
lit from within
float in the night radio

22

thunder bangs our heads together
daylight inside out
the hedgehog clenched in her prickles

23
in the saved student newspaper my idiot truth letter:
'O widen the circle!
– above all non-hierarchical'

24
the pitbull ate a hedgehog
and a cat
we had to get rid of it

25
think what to write
scrub mould off the bathroom ceiling
spores released

26
drawn to walk the wetland path
remote enough for the man's attack – fly you pūkekos! raised on wings of fear
i'd not forgive myself

27
our war dead
their imperial invasion at Gallipoli defeated
lest we forget

28
Issa haiku
mine that world
lumps of coal on the fire

29
cleaning: so they see you
don't own it
leave some shit

30
two of us going on can use the truck lane
makes us quicker than the rest
in the motorway's fog pillows

31
they'll know
while Earth burned
we fiddled with our nature poems

32
street sleepers
car windows obscured
with white breath nets

33
as i drive off
you step into the lift
each with our secrets

34
rain makes a song and dance about the washing
the door blows shut on the cat's tail
she howls to finish it

35
is that you? in the phone
or in the fine gold chain i lie along the ledge of my screen
all of a piece it spills

36
eat an egg from an uncaged hen
my eggs are gone
so my cluckiness

37
i don't want to crawl along the hall
wiping dirt off the skirting board
– in a total eclipse if it's Serie scrubbing out the sun i might

38
not all the poems can be written in winter
libraries have them
we longed all summer for this rain

39

bakery slice
if the Doc is pleased with my cholesterol
i'll make it

40

how about leaving an extra line between?
but you don't
ah – the quick step

41

some monkey crumb i pick up
and eat
fortunately sweet

42

the hurt cat fled
– that's her!
a soccer ball on the verandah

43

every
thing i knitted says my mum
casting on for my daughter

44

those freezer-burned peas dumped in the grass
birds come down in the rain and peck out the innards
pale shells left

45

hardly older than i and dying of 'natural' causes
once-in-sixty-years weather events
every fortnight

46

'Saint Paul?' says Ila – 'a gay man in denial'
emptying compost under the dripping plum
my bare feet take a joyful chill

47
pristine toe shoes in the Sally Army window
season's end
satin sausages to barbeque the feet en pointe

48
Chen Li's poems' sense before us
the phrases unsettled: make
for a threshold – word-quake

49
she's run out of inhalants
we can't breathe
on the drive to casualty she gasps: 'you don't need – to be silent'

50
pots simmer
stars wheel
abjure letters to the editor

51
rain speaks sharply
to razed cliff tops: No!
No! to shaved riverbanks

52
read 'our dark Dunedin houses'
in Cilla's shifts of light
honey to the cave of cold hands

53
leaf raking the trees tell me
everything
about winter

54
in the language changing rooms of Michele's poems
i don't know where to look
hot showers on a cold day: cold showers in the heat

55
men's clean lineages
muddied with women's names
'step away from the tree!'

56
and luxuriate in this unforgivable sin:
translating your poem
to mean what i wish

57
this camellia
takes no prisoners: all the fallen
rotting at its feet

58
in sheds
on the net: men watching
i watch the milk

59
rain beats on the house
puffs of heat escape the blankets
the cup of cold tea knocked into my bedside drawer

60
from the sunken pool our little one lifted: alive
the baby wobbling across the coastal highway – a passing driver scoops her up
gives back this holiday of a lifetime our last resort

61
on the racecourse i find the nine of clubs
what kind of luck is this? the pack thrown off – i'm away
mountains fold into the ocean forgotten shopping lists

62
hoist in pale sky: one lemon cloud – the horizon firing a gold line
winter hitting on her
that fourteen-week stand down for the dole

63
pain in my heels and wrists
three emails
back to bed – all the answers winged in sleep

64
is there anything you're afraid to find a way to say?
here when they break the social contract
anyone who has them on about it gets accused of the politics of envy

65
dishes tower in the sink: cutlery propped in a dirty pot: glasses rounded up
off the coast oil rigs suck: illegals sunk
wage earners prop up bankers' profits: run in the hot

66
my dream
has
deep pockets

67
sun-up at this landing window i watch
the neighbour child across the close
in his cot a-bounce

68
all the US texts i've read referencing each other
whippoorwills and chickadees with the chirpy authority of tray-liners
– throw away the wings thrashing in my hands – my head jerked back

69
those amber those carnelian wrist beads
cheap beyond belief
live ammunition from the faraway market

70

shoes off shoes on: i enter your poems
living things
make me ashamed of my possessions

71

i'm to take my daughter for a driving lesson
the other time there was a little crash
today the anger melts away from us

72

he prefers her oblivious
to the adulation
sweated from her pores like last night's garlic

73

washing pegged out
rain or shine drier
millennia of women eyeing the sky

74

The Menstrual School is taking enrolments
fees by monthly direct debit
on open day we walk across the playing-field arm in arm with our mates

75

a cop car: three get out
one to the back one to the front: she knocks
one waits under the bedroom window – of the empty house

76

in the receiving line
fearing they'll hongi
fearing they won't

77

trestle tables under tarpaulins raised the length of the driveway
dark windows open: inside voices
arm deep in the hedge a woman cutting camellias

78
at the station the maquis approach: 'but how did you know me?'
– led through back streets: 'tell anyone this address and they'll come for us'
but in the safe house it's just women and their kids

79
reaching
the glass sealing
– her print ride's off

80
more in sorrow than in anger or they go for the jugular
that teacherly reviewer: 'commend recommend commend'
best of all a call from the back of the cave – where prance shadowy figures

81
Diana gives me a little jug
both bridges pour from it: 'the orange of enlightenment'
'a pink to sear the senses'

82
my psychotic break:
trios of cans
in health-ticked shrink-wrap

83
how i praise her in that report
next term she announces her engagement
driving with the handbrake on

84
somewhere in these clothes an insect
biting across my belly
makes me itch for unguents and fresh linen

85
TV rap channel on low: he watches her
pick something good to eat from the tree
there it is! Disobedience

86
a visitor coming: if it's my mother i'll clean the hand basins
the house smells of soup
do i offer an explanation?

87
if hers is foreplay his is afterplay
should it come to a third act
they'll breathe in the anticipatory hush of the auditorium

88
i can't get blood out of a stone
but i can
get blood out of a towel

89
man on deck
explaining rainbow science
to his sons

90
a trippy instrumental
freezes in the headlights:
Morning Report

91
PD boys in hazard fluoros
rakes   leaf blower
loppers   secateurs

92
Uncle & Mr
& Mrs Duck – down again for the shooting season
i lay out fresh crusts

93
like something from *Modern Girls' Annual*
dinner-plate fungi have sprouted under the shrubs
Hillary and Monica get wasted

94
'Could what she's saying be true? – we'll never know.'
kind sir you bet your sweet arse
we do

95
what's passed between us:
kuaka shadows speed across the grass
a brimming instant in their wings

96
at any window with the light behind me
a gunshot
clears my head

97
try to press the spot
on my conscience
where i just squeak past

98
in the foyer to be devoured
two cardboard boxes full of fruit
their teacher's marked every leaf every stalk every bruise

99
where the mower blade missed
a fluke: one bladder of spring onion
breaks above the turf

100
the tulip
stem collapsed
i cut it short and stick it in a little bottle with a sprig of heather

101
make of the feminine voice
a truce a trace
induce green leaf

Acknowledgements

This collection was started during a 2009 residency at the International Writers' Workshop held annually at Hong Kong Baptist University. A further draft was completed during a guest readership at the 2014 Taipei International Poetry Forum. Grateful thanks to the organisers of these events.

Thanks also to the editors of *Brief*, *Ka Mate Ka Ora: A New Zealand journal of poetry and poetics*, *Kokako*, *Landfall*, *Mascara* and *New Kiwi Women Write Their Stories* in which some of these poems have previously appeared. A version of '101 snapshots' – a response to *Microcosmos*, the untraditional haiku of Chen Li – appeared as part of 'All Together Now: A digital bridge for Auckland and Sydney' at the nzepc. 'of our lucky eight' can be heard online at: www.nzepc.auckland.ac.nz/features/six-pack-sound/

The definition of 仁 in the poem of the same name is cited in Linda W.L. Young (1994), *Crosstalk and Culture in Sino-American Communication*, Cambridge University Press, Cambridge, New York and Melbourne, p. 109.

The title 'to *my* room nineteen' references the short story 'To Room Nineteen' by Doris Lessing. The titles 'And leaned my head. I, too, had praise for your book …' and 'What is it makes the stranger?' and the introductory note for '101 snapshots' are from Robin Hyde's 'Fragments From Two Countries'.

About the author

Janet Charman has published seven previous poetry collections. The most recent, *At the White Coast* (AUP, 2012), is a memoir of a year working in London during the Thatcher era. The manuscript of that collection was joint winner of the 2010 International Writers' Workshop Kathleen Grattan Prize for a Previously Unpublished Sequence of Poems. Her collection *Cold Snack* (AUP, 2007) won the poetry prize at the Montana New Zealand Book Awards in 2008. She has an MA in English from the University of Auckland, where she tutored New Zealand literature for several years and was their 1997 writer in residence. Charman trained as a general and maternity nurse on leaving high school and has also worked in secondary teaching. She lives in Auckland with her partner and their two daughters.